Some Remarks Upon Mr. Church's Vindication of Miraculous Powers, &c. With an Observation or two Upon Dr. Stebbing's Christianity Justified, ... In a Letter to a Friend. By F. Toll,

SOME
REMARKS

UPON

Mr. *Church*'s Vindication

OF

MIRACULOUS POWERS, *&c.*

(Price One Shilling.)

SOME
REMARKS

UPON

Mr. *Church*'s Vindication

OF

MIRACULOUS POWERS, &c.

WITH

An OBSERVATION or TWO

UPON

Dr. STEBBING's *Christianity Justified,*

So far as relates to this Subject.

In a LETTER to a FRIEND.

By *F. TOLL*, M. A.
Rector of *Dogmersfield, Hampshire.*

LONDON
Printed for J SHUCKBURGH, between the
Temple-Gates, in *Fleet-Street.*
M DCC L.

SOME

REMARKS, &c.

S I R,

OUT of Regard to your Perfuafion, I have looked over Mr. *Church*'s Work in Vindication of the *Miraculous Powers,* &c. and, notwithftanding the folemn Approbation it has received fiom a learned Univerfity, muft take the Liberty to fay, it is far from giving me Satisfaction upon the Queftion in debate. Whatever Learning or good Senfe there may be in the

B   Book,

Book, I cannot avoid thinking it deficient in the main Article, that of Proof. I am not formed to pay a blind Deference to the Judgment of any Man, or Body of Men, whatfoever; I cannot acquiefce in a Decifion, however formidable made by Numbers, where my own Reafon is not fatisfied. Thofe learned Gentlemen, by whom Freedom of Thought will ever be efteemed a moft valuable Privilege, will therefore forgive me, if, for once, I differ in Opinion from them, and fairly acknowledge, that Mr. *Church* has not removed thofe Doubts, which Dr. *Middleton*'s Performance had raifed in my Mind. —— To remark upon all the Particulars of this Work, would be to write a large Volume, which it is not my Intention to do. I fhall only throw together a few general Obfervations, in Support of my Opinion, and leave you to difpofe of them, according to the Weight you fhall think them of.

With refpect to thofe who are diftinguifhed by the Title of *Apoftolical Fathers,*

Fathers, and whom Dr. *Middleton* affirms
to have made " no Claim or Pretenfion,
" in all their feveral Pieces, to any of
" thofe extraordinary Gifts, which are
" the Subject of this Enquiry," I can
difcover nothing in what is produced by
Mr. *Church* to invalidate this Affirmation.
He does not pretend to fay, they have
related, or pointed at, any particular Facts
as Inftances of this Power; (except in the
Cafe of Vifions, *&c.* which I fhall take
Notice of prefently;) and thofe Paffages
which he has fingled out, as containing
plain Allufions to it, have, I think, been
fhewn by very rational Arguments, (as
yet unanfwered) fome quite incapable of
being underftood in the Senfe of alluding
to them, the others manifeftly capable of
another Acceptation, and, upon the whole,
that no indifferent Enquirer would ever
collect a Notion of the Exiftence of any
fuch Powers from the Paffages themfelves.
Upon the Word χάρισμα no Strefs ought
to be laid; it is plain and evident the
Apoftolical Fathers made Ufe of it in an

unre-

unreftrained Senfe, and therefore nothing certain upon the Point in difpute can pofﬁbly be concluded from it.

With refpect to the Viﬁons and private Revelations which thefe holy Men pretend to, and which Mr. *Church* feems to mention as of fome Moment, they appear to me, whether true or falfe, quite foreign to the prefent Purpofe; and I cannot imagine but this Writer muﬅ be of the fame Opinion alfo, if he only carries his Eye a little downwards, and takes in the latter Part of Dr. *Middleton*'s Paragraph, (recited in Part before) which we find expreffed in thefe Words : " Nor to any " ﬅanding Power of working Miracles, as " refiding ﬅill among them, for the Con- " verfion of the heathen World." Which laﬅ Words are plainly applicable to each Branch of the Paragraph ; becaufe whatever *Gifts* are not to be confidered as relative to this End, are not worth difputing about. Now *Viﬁons* and *Revelations*, unfupported by any other Evidence, what-

ever

ever they may be to a Man's felf, are certainly no Proof at all to another Perfon : They could have no Effect towards the *Converfion of the heathen World*, and therefore they need not heie have been urged againft Dr. *Middleton*, whofe Meaning common Equity will confine to fuch *Gifts*, as thofe who poffeffed them, could give fome Demonftration of to the ieft of Mankind.

Befides, thefe Vifions and Revelations aie very uncertain Things in themfelves, and very little to be depended on : We have heard of veiy good, yea, and very fenfible Men too, who have miftaken their own warm Imaginations for divine Illuminations, and the immediate Operations of the Holy Spirit. Was a Man to tell me he had been warned of fuch a Thing in a Vifion, or he had received fuch a Doctrine immediately from Heaven, whatever my Opinion of his Goodnefs might be, I fhould not think myfelf obliged to believe him upon his baie Affirmation, becaufe,

becaufe, without an Intention of deceiving me, he may poffibly be deceived himfelf. I think I fhould have a Right to require fome furthei Manifeftation of a fuper-natural Intercourfe, and, in Defeƈt of fuch Manifeftation, to fufpend my Affent.

For thefe Reafons I cannot but be a good deal furprized to fee fo great a Strefs laid upon the *Vifions* of *Hermas.* If they are what they pretend to be, they con-clude nothing againft the *Free Enquiry*, for the Reafon above-given, becaufe their Influence could not extend beyond his own Perfon. I fhould be glad to be informed, if thofe Gentlemen who think proper to argue from thefe *Vifions*, do really believe the Writer to have been infpired, or not? If they are in Truth infpired, pray, ought they not to be fet upon a Level with the other acknowledged Scriptures, and read in our Churches now, as Hiftory informs us they once weie? It can never be right, that fuch a Slight fhould pafs upon any Part of God's Word. But if thefe Vifions

were

were not from Heaven, what Weight are they of? For my Part, I fee no Medium between Infpired and Uninfpired, they are either the Work of God, or the Work of Man; if of Man, they are then upon the fame Foot with other human Compofitions of the fame Nature, that is, with the Compofitions of other enthufiaftick Vifionaries, for in that Light only, to fpeak the Truth, I can confider them. The Stories of the *young Lady* and the *old Lady* are of fuch a peculiar Caft, as to put one very much in Mind of the *Fairy Tales*. I fhould not fpeak of this primitive Piece in fo contemptuous a Manner, if I was not myfelf convinced, upon what appear to me clear Principles of Reafon, that the Spirit of God had nothing to do with it. The Ground of my Perfuafion is this: I can admit no Doctrine to come from God, that, in any Point, contradicts the Doctrine delivered by our Saviour. Now this is fo evidently the Cafe, with refpect to the Vifions of *Hermos*, that 'tis a Wonder no Notice

fhould

fhould be taken of it, by thofe who have made Ufe of their Authority, in the Courfe of this Controverfy. It is the profeffed Bufinefs of one of the Chapters to fhew that it is unlawful for a Man, who is divorced from his Wife, even for the Caufe of Adultery, to marry again; in exprefs Contradiction to our Saviour, *Matt.* xix. 9. where the Liberty of marrying again under thofe Circumftances is manifeftly allowed. I muft crave Leave to look upon this as a fure Way of judging upon this Occafion, a fure Way of trying the Pretences of a Revelation: If it contains any Thing inconfiftent with *one* we are already poffeffed of, and know to have been delivered us from Heaven, this Inconfiftency is, in my Eftimation, an infallible Mark of its Falfhood. And it makes no Difference whether this appears in an hundred Inftances, or only in one; the Authority of Chrift is not to be controverted in a fingle Point; whatever Writing does this at all, whether in more Inftances or fewer, whether the Product of the firft Century

or

or the eighteenth, I look upon as entitled to no Manner of Regard, nor shall it ever receive any Reverence from me.

There is one Argument more which I must just touch upon in this Place. Dr. *Middleton* had asserted, that these Fathers *made no Claim, in all their several Pieces, to any extraordinary Gifts,* &c. and thence inferred a Probability that there was no such Thing. Mr. *Church* is of Opinion this Inference is not just, he argues that there is very little Mention of miraculous Gifts in the Epistles of the Apostles, it does not hence follow that there was no such Thing, because we know that there was, the Silence therefore of the Apostles being allowed to be no Argument against the Existence of miraculous Gifts in their Days, why must it be admitted as a better Argument against the Existence of the same Gifts, in the Days of their Successors ? To this we say, that altho', in some of these Epistles, there is no Mention at all made of these Gifts, yet we have a cotemporary

C   Rela-

Relation of feveral particular Facts being performed by the fame Perfons who wrote the Epiftles, which affures us of their Exiftence, and upon which our Faith in them is founded, which is the Circumftance we want in the latter Cafe : And it will not, I prefume, be afferted, that, if there was no hiftorical Account given us of any Commiffion to the Apoftles to work Miracles, or of any Miracles really wrought by them, it could be proved from thofe Epiftles where no Mention is made of them, there were any fuch Powers in Being. We may therefore, as Things are, very reafonably doubt of the latter, for the fame Reafon as we fhould doubt of the former, had we received no pofitive Information concerning them. The great Probability that, if Miracles had been wrought after the Apoftles Times, fome Hiftory of them would have been delivered down to future Ages, has already been fuggefted in the Courfe of this Difpute, and I muft continue to think this Suggeftion carries fome Weight in it, 'till I fee it confuted.

futed. Providence either did intend them
for our Use, or it did not, if it did, they
would have been tranfmitted to us upon
better Authority; if it did not, there may
be an End of Difpute, we need trouble our
Heads but very little about them.

I cannot be fatisfied with Mr. *Church*'s
Account of *Polycarp*'s Martyrdom. He
fuppofes the whole Circumftance of the
Dove to have been an Interpolation, firft
conducted by Tradition into the Margin,
and then re-inferted, by fome Tranfcriber,
into the Text. He founds this Suppofition
upon the Authority of *Eufebius*, who, in
giving an Account of this Affair, makes
not the leaft Mention of the *Dove*'s Part
in it.—This is not fufficient for me; for,
in the firft Place, I do not fee how fuch
an odd Particular fhould get into the Margin, if no Hint had been given by the firft
Relators, befides, I cannot entirely reft
upon *Eufebius* in this Matter, he feems to
me to have taken fome Pains in fmoothing
the whole Story over, in order to render

it

it more credible than he found it: He
was not willing quite to lose the Miracle,
and could no otherwise preserve it, than
by dropping some Circumstances, and
softening others, and this, whoever com-
pares his Method of relating it, with the
original Letter translated by Archbishop
Wake, will, I think, be convinced was
the Truth of the Case. I wonder to find
Mr. *Church* affirming, " the only Miracle
" here, is the Circumstance of the *Dove*;"
so point-blank contrary to the whole Tenor
of the Letter, which plainly relates all the
other Circumstances, of the Voice from
Heaven, the fragrant Odour that issued
from his Body, and the great Effusion of
Blood, as miraculous. Of the last it is
particularly said, that it " raised an Ad-
" miration in all the People." As well
indeed it might, for it is an Effect every
Tittle as surprizing, and as much above
the common Course of Nature, as any
other that can be described. I can, for
my own Part, as easily conceive a Pigeon's
Nest in the good Bishop's Belly, as that his

Body

Body should contain Blood enough to extinguish a large Fire, or that a large Fire should be extinguished by two or three Gallons, the utmost Quantity that an human Body is allowed to contain So that, putting the Story of the Dove quite out of the Question, this Particular remains still to be accounted for, and, 'till it is accounted for in a better Way than I have yet seen, I must be obliged to look upon it as such an Incumbrance upon the Narrative, as will justify my refusing a compleat Assent to it. I will here take Leave to add this one general Observation ; that those Writers appear to me to entertain very low, unworthy Notions of the supreme Being, who can thus suppose him exerting his Almighty Power in shewing of Tricks; for no better a Name do many of those wonderous Works deserve, which some learned Divines would impose upon our Belief, as almost of Necessity to Salvation.

I pro-

I proceed to fay a Word upon the Cafe of *Autolichus* and *Theophilus*, wherein I am not at all enlightened by Mr. *Church's* Labours. He feems to have adopted Mr. *Dodwell's* Reafoning upon this Article, and therefore it will not be amifs to examine a little what that Gentleman had offered in Explanation of it. I had omitted to enlarge at all upon it in my Remarks upon the *Free Anfwer*, from an Apprehenfion that it might have been deemed an Infult upon the common Senfe of my Readers, to take up their Time in fetting afide an Interpretation of a Paffage, that every Man muft fee to be falfe by the flighteft Attention to the Paffage itfelf. But fometimes, we perceive, it happens, that plain Words are to go for nothing. I do not undertake to travel with thefe Gentlemen into the Depths of Learning. All I pretend to, is a moderate Proportion of plain Senfe and Reafon, and a Knowledge enough of the learned Languages to preferve my Faculties from being puzzled and confounded by what

what is called the Learning of other Men.
———But to the Bufinefs. The Author of
the *Free Anfwer* firft fuppofes, that *Autolichus* required to fee *Theophilus* raife a dead
Perfon to Life in his Prefence. A Suppofition without the Colour of a Reafon for
its Support. I will take upon me to affert,
that a Man might write a Volume as big
as a Church Bible, and never be able to
prove, that, δεῖξόν μοι κἂν ἕνα ἐγερθέντα ἐκ
νεκρῶν, fignifies Let me fee you raife a
Perfon from the dead ; ἕνα ἐγερθέντα, when
its Meaning is not perverted or darkened
by Criticifm, fignifies one *Raifed*, or one
that *has been raifed*, and not one in the
very Article of Rifing. *Autolichus*'s Demand in plain *Englifh* is this : Shew me
one that has been raifed from the Dead,
and I will believe. Now what are the
Steps *Theophilus* takes, when put to this
Teft ? Thofe who judge after the Manner
of Men, might naturally expect he would
omit nothing in his Power to gain a Perfon
the moft indifferent to him over to the
Chriftian Religion , and that he would be
in

in a ftill higher Degree concerned for a
Friend, as *Autolichus* is reprefented to have
been. Thus, I fay, would Charity prompt
every good Man to act upon the com-
moneft Occafion of this Nature, and Charity
is obferved to operate with double Force,
when improved and heightened by particular Affections. We may conclude,
then, the good Bifhop would not fail to
give his Friend all the Satisfaction it was
in his Power to do. We may very
rationally fuppofe him to have replied to
this Effect: Perhaps you may expect to
fee me raife a Perfon to Life in your Prefence; but, I muft inform you, this your
Expectation is not founded in Reafon.
Tho' the fupreme Being may have granted
this Power to me, yet it is a Power which
he will not fuffer to be fported with, or
wantonly exerted at every one's Call, juft
to gratify a vain and idle Curiofity; but
to be produced only at fuch Times, and
upon fuch Occafions, as, in his great
Wifdom, he fhall think worthy of fuch
an Interpofition, of which Times and
Occafions

Occasions no Man can be, and he only is, an adequate Judge. For the same Reason you are not to expect to see this great Work performed with your own Eyes by any other Person whatsoever ; but altho' this Sort of Evidence be not to be afforded you, because it cannot be commanded at Pleasure, yet we are able to produce you such as ought fully to satisfy a reasonable Enquirer. We are able to produce you Instances of Persons now living, who have been dead, and that they have been dead, we are ready to give you all the Proof, that the Nature of the Thing will admit of, or that any Man willing to be convinced can ingenuously require. No Man can deny that this is a Fact capable of being satisfactorily proved, who allows the Truth of any Fact that did not immediately fall under the Cognizance of his own Senses.

Had the Power of raising the Dead, or any Remains and Footsteps of this Power, then subsisted, I candidly ask, could *The-*

D   *ophilus*

opli'us have done lefs towards the Converfion of his Fiiend, than is heie fet forth?
Would not Dr. *Dodwell*, Mi. *Church*, or
any other good Man, at this Time have
pioceeded in this Method? But let us fee
what Reply is in Fact made. Why truly
this: " If I fhould fhew you one raifed
" from the Dead, and ftill living, even
" this you would difbelieve." By the
Way, a direct Confutation of the firft Suppofition, the Words, *ftill living*, plainly
impoiting, that the Perfon *Autolichus* de-
fired to fee alive, might have been raifed
fiom the Dead fome Diftance of Time
before. From his own Woids, before recited, it is as manifeft as the Sun at Noon-
day, that he did not requiie to fee a Man
brought to Life in his Prefence, and from
this Reply, that *Theophilus* did not under-
ftand him fo. But, which ever Way this
be determined, the Anfwer was furely a
very ftrange one, and veiy unworthy a
Chriftian Bifhop. I defire to be informed
how *Theophilus* could know, that this fenfible Heathen would ftill continue dif-
believing?

believing? He could not poſſibly be ſure what Influence and Effect this Miracle might have upon his Heart, and therefore, if he had any Evidence to produce, I muſt inſiſt, not only that the Thing would have been natural, but that it would have been ſtrictly incumbent upon him, in Point of Duty, as well as of Friendſhip, to have laid it before him. There is no Parallel between this Caſe, and what happened at our Saviour's Crucifixion, when the *Jews* declared, if *he would come down from the Croſs, they would believe*, becauſe our Saviour did infallibly know, how the Miracle would operate upon thoſe who required it; *Theophilus* did not, and therefore it was his Buſineſs to try. And ſince in Fact he did not try, or make any Attempt towards the Conviction of his Friend, in a Point where his Welfare was ſo deeply concerned, Reaſon will juſtify us in concluding, that the Power pretended to was at this Time withdrawn, and all Marks and Effects of it entirely worn out.

D 2

But

But after having, by his Approbation, made Mr. *Dodwell's* Reasoning his own, Mr. *Church* goes on, and makes this suitable Addition : " However, it must be " owned, that *Autolichus's* Demand was " unreasonable." Against this I enter my Protest aloud, That indeed he has found People to *own* it, we confess, and think it should be registered among the lucky Incidents of the Gentleman's Life : But, to distinguish myself from all such easy Approvers, I declare, that to me the *Demand* appears the most reasonable Thing in the World. There is the highest Probability that, in their Conversations upon these Subjects, *Theophilus* had made some Mention of such Powers residing amongst the Christians. What more natural, I will say, what more reasonable for a Doubter to urge upon this Occasion, than this, Pray, give me some Proof, shew me an Instance of the Power you claim, and I will believe ? I affirm the Reply to have been natural, fair, and ingenuous. But suppose it was not, allow the Demand to have been un-reasonable, what then ? Does it hence

fol-

follow that it was not very fit and reasonable for *Theophilus* to endeavour at giving his Friend all the Satisfaction he was able? Most certainly no A Demand may be very unreasonable on the Part of him who makes it, at the same Time that it may be very right and expedient for a Man to afford a serious Answer to it, especially if it be modestly proposed, and upon such a Subject as Religion, then, I say, Reason, Truth, and Charity strictly require this Return at our Hands. But the Reason Mr. *Church* assigns why this Demand was unreasonable is still better : "Because there were " other very sufficient Arguments to have " satisfied him of the Truth of Christianity." This is exactly what I myself would say; I am of quite the same Opinion. But I am afraid this Gentleman will find, upon a Review, that the Concession here made is not altogether consistent with the general Design of his Undertaking. For, if there were other Arguments sufficient to convince *Autolichus*, I presume the same may be judged sufficient to convince another Person ; and if another, then many; and

if

if many, then all. So that the *Neceffity*
of Miracles is at this Rate entirely fet afide.
Thofe who defend a Miracle, argue upon
the Prefumption of its being neceffary, becaufe God can never be fuppofed to exert
his Power in an extraoidinary Manner,
when the End in View may as well be at-
tained without it. Upon Mr. *Church*'s own
Principles, no Neceffity for Miracles; the
Confequence unavoidable, therefore none.
I beg Mr. *Chuich*'s Paidon, for thinking
that they who are fo ftrenuous in the Defence of thefe latter Miracles, whatever
Honour they may do the Fathers, pay no
very great Compliment to the Chriftian
Religion. Had it no Strength of its own?
No intrinfick Excellence? Nothing in its
own Nature to recommend it to the *Reafon*
of Mankind? It has always been thought
that there was fomething extraoidinary in
the Propagation of the Gofpel in the firft
Ages; and, upon the Suppofition that it
was in fome Meafure left to itfelf, left to
work its own Way, only by Application of
the firft Miracles, and the Excellence of
its Doctrines, no Doubt but there was:
But

But if it be fuppofed that the Hand of God fo vifibly attended it in every Step it made thro' fo many Centuries, that the Almighty made bare his Arm, and upheld it by a Power every Moment evident to Mens Senfes, I fincerely confefs there appears to my Eyes nothing more marvellous in the Progrefs it made, than there does that the Religion of *Mahomet* fhould be univerfally eftablifhed in the *Turkifh* Empire by Dint of the Sword.

Mr. *Church* profeffes to vindicate the Miracles of the three firft Centuries only. Whatever is without the Limits of this Period, he has therefore kept himfelf perfectly clear of, but whatever falls within the faid Compafs, feems to be a neceffary Part of his Concern. For this Reafon I cannot but think it a little ftrange, that we find no Notice taken, nor the leaft Mention made of *Gregory Thaumatergus*, tho' he is a good deal infifted upon in the *Free Enquiry.*——— This Father flourifhed in the Middle of the third Century, and there

are

are great Variety of Miracles recorded of his working. How is a Man to receive thefe Miracles? Am I to believe them, or am I not? What Direction does our Author give in this Matter? What, not a Word to recommend him? Not a Syllable in his Favour? How am I to account for this Omiffion? Some Reafon for fuch a profound Silence affuredly there muft be; I will not take upon me to determine with Precifion what that Reafon was; however I will affume the Liberty of indulging a Conjecture, that their Abfurdities are fo glaring, and at the fame Time the Authorities for their Truth fo ftrong and unqueftionable, that Mr. *Church*, tho' fo able a Vindicator, did not well know how to difpofe of them, and therefore chofe the fecurer Way of drawing a Veil over the Object, that it might as little as poffible be expofed to vulgar Infpection. We have the fame Obfervation to make concerning the Miracles of the *Monk Anthony*; I fuppofe him to have lived towards the latter End of the third Century, as his Life and Works are

recorded

recorded by that great Man St. *Athanafius,*
who is faid to have feen him with his own
Eyes, and whofe Relation of Facts is,
without Doubt, as little to be difputed as
his Explanation of Doctrines.

Should Mr *Church* reply to this, that,
altho' the Miracles of *Thaumatergus* and
Anthony the Monk be indeed the Miracles
of the third Century, yet that they are
come down to us only upon the Authority
of Writers in the fourth, (which I apprehend muft be the Retreat) I fhould then
take it as a Favour to be informed, whether
this Author does really believe the Accounts of thefe Miracles himfelf? If he
does not, (as I am willing to judge may be
the Cafe) I fhould be glad to fee, upon a
Paper before me, fairly and diftinctly upon
what Grounds he rejects them The Life
of the former, in which many furprizing
Stories are told, is writ by St. *Bafil* and
Gregory of *Nyffa,* that of the latter, containing Events equally wonderful, (as was
faid before) by *Athanafius,* Men, it muft

E   be

be allowed, as renowned, and who made as great a Figure in the Church, as any that went before them. To thefe we will add the *Saints Chryfoftom*, *Jerom*, and *Auftin*, great Names, and all of the fourth Century! It is generally thought they were fuperior in Learning to moft of their Predeceffors, and we muft not prefume to think they were any Way inferior in their moral Characters. Thefe have each of them given fome Hiftory of Miracles either in or juft preceding their own Times, wherein they have not contented them-felves with general Affirmations, but come more home to the Point, launching forth into the Defcription of particular Facts. But the Misfortune is, they came a Century too late, and therefore muft have no Credit. We are allowed to proceed to the very Boundaries of the third, but—ftop— The fourth is all a Land of Deception; the next Step is full into the Territories of Error and Falfhood. But whence this great Difference, I wonder, for, to my Shame be it fpoken, as yet I do not under-ftand.

ftand. This appears to be one of the main Difficulties in the Queftion ; a Solution has more than once been called for, but none is yet afforded. How is a plain, well-meaning Man to conduct himfelf under this Dilemma? Had Mr. *Church*'s Book laid down any certain Principle that would enable me to make a juft Diftinction in this Matter, *viz.* between the Degrees of Credit that are refpectively due to each of thefe neighbouring Centuries, it would have much greater Weight with me than it has at prefent.

To ftate my Objections to this large Work in few Words.——They ftand thus.

The Author has not proved to my Satisfaction that the Chriftian Writers of the firft Century after the Apoftles, have either made exprefs Mention of any miraculous Powers as then exifting in the Church, or even clearly referred to them.

He

He hath not ſhewn that the following
Writers who do ſpeak of them as ex-
iſting, tho' they were Men of the greateſt
Eminence, and the greateſt Lights of the
Church, either poſſeſſed theſe Powers
themſelves in any Degree, or were ever
Eye-Witneſſes of their being exerciſed by
any other Perſons.

The only particular Miracle he has un-
dertaken to defend within the whole Com-
paſs of his three Centuries, (having, I
think, dropped the Caſe of *Proculus* and
Severus) is what is ſaid to have happened
at the Martyrdom of *Polycarp*. But the
moſt genuine Account we have of this
Affair labours with Difficulties of which
the utmoſt Efforts of his Learning have
not yet diſcarded it. Upon the Footing
he has left the Story, the ſeveral abſurd
Circumſtances, wholly unaccounted for,
render it, ſo far as my Reaſon enables me
to judge, quite incredible.——Surely it muſt
be thought a Thing extraordinary that an
Advocate

Advocate for the Doctrine, that Miracles were commonly wrought in the Church for the Space of Three Hundred Years, should be able to fix but upon one single Fact, and not be able to prove that Fact beyond all reasonable Doubt and Contradiction. Does not hence a Probability arise that he is only an Advocate for a Suppposition ? — To go on.

I see no Reason the Author could have for waving all Mention of *Gregory* the Wonder-Worker, but a Consciousnefs that the Miracles recorded of him are indefensible, and that no Teftimony barely human can fufficiently recommend them to the Belief of Mankind.

Laftly, There is no competent Reason affigned, why we are to believe that miraculous Powers were continued to the Church juft three Centuries and no longer. That they were neceffary 'till Chriftianity gained an Eftablifhment by the Converfion of the Civil Powers, and that their Neceffity

ceffity then ceafed, is a bare Conjecture, unfupported by any Proof or Authority whatfoever. Was there any fufficient Teftimony of the Fact, that Miracles did continue fo long, and then ceafed, this might be affignable as a Reafon for it, but there is no arguing to a Fact from a fuppofed Neceffity, Facts are to be proved by direct Evidence, and not by Suppofition. If there be any real Difference, in Point of Credibility, between the Miracles of the third and fourth Centuries, this Difference muft arife from fome fuppofed Difference in the Characters of the Writers who flourished in thofe Times, and upon whofe Authority they are delivered down to us. Now if there be any Thing better or worfe in the Characters of the Writers, the Advantage confeffedly lies on the Side of the latter. If they were fuperior in Learning, and equal in Judgment and Integrity, to thofe who had gone before them, which is the general Opinion, their Accounts will feem rather to demand a higher Degree of Credit. But Mr. *Church* allows us to reject thefe Accounts

counts of a later Date, which Allowance
I would willingly accept of; tho', upon
the ftrictteft Enquiry, I can difcover no Argument for rejecting *them*, but what lies
ftronger againft all thofe he is fo induftrious
to vindicate. If there be any fure Mark
of Diftinction in this Cafe, and the
Gentleman had it in View, he would
have done well to produce it, for the Be-
nefit of thofe, whofe Unhappinefs it is to be
lefs difcerning than himfelf.——Thus much
for Mr. *Church.*

You will not, I imagine, think it im-
pertinent, if I lengthen my Letter with
an Obfervation or two upon what I find
advanced by Dr. *Stebbing,* relative to this
Subject, in his *Boyle*'s Lectures lately pub-
lifhed.——In the firft Place, I hope this
learned and ingenious Writer will pardon
me for being of Opinion, that it can be of
no Ufe to the Caufe he is engaged in, *viz.*
the Defence of Chriftianity, to be over
hafty in pointing out the Advantages
which Dr. *Middleton*'s Argument may
afford

afford to Unbelievers. I fhould think it better to leave this Matter patiently to Unbelievers themfelves. There is an old Saying at a Game upon the Dice, that a Blot is no Blot 'till 'tis hit. There feems to be no Occafion to direct an Enemy to the Weakneffes in our Fortification, this may be deemed at leaft Officioufnefs, if not Folly. We need not lend our Affiftance; let Unbelievers explore for themfelves: Poffibly they may overlook this Advantage, however, if they do not, it will be Time enough to defend, when the Attack is begun. For my own Part, I declare myfelf quite eafy upon this Head; and this Eafe proceeds, not I truft, from any Coldnefs or neutral Difpofition towards the Chriftian Religion, but from a thorough Conviction that Unbelievers will not find an Inch of Ground yielded up to them, which ever Way this Difpute fhall at laft turn. My Reafon is fully fatisfied and perfuaded, that the Gofpel Miracles may as well be defended upon the Principles of the *Free Enquiry*, as ever they were before; and,

and, if *they* ſtand good, the Chriſtian
Religion is out of Danger : If any Unbeliever ſhall hereafter ariſe, weak enough
to think otherwiſe, and purſue his fooliſh
Opinion into Practice, I will venture to
propheſy the Experiment will be attended
with no worſe Conſequence than expoſing
himſelf, I queſtion not but a great Number of Pens will be found ready to give
a reaſonable and ſolid Anſwer to any Thing
he ſhall be able to bring out againſt them.
To enter a little into Particulars.

Dr. *Middleton* had ſaid, that, tho' " we
" have no Doubt of St. *Polycarp*'s Mar-
" tyrdom, yet we may reaſonably pauſe at
" the Miracles which are ſaid to have at-
" tended it," &c. Dr. *Stebbing* aſks why
an Unbeliever may not, by the ſame Argument, go on and ſay, " tho' we admit
" the Narrative of the Life and Death of
" Jeſus Chriſt, yet we pauſe at the Mira-
" cles which are ſaid to have been wrought
" in his Favour, either when he was living,
" or after he was dead, &c." It appears

F   won-

wonderful to me, that a Man of Dr. *Stebbing*'s Penetration fhould put thefe two
Cafes upon a Level, between which there
is fo wide and apparent a Difference. That
a Man may with great Sincerity *paufe* at
the former, and not at the latter, I know
to be poffible, becaufe it is the exact Situa-
tion of my own Mind at the Inftant I write
this. I do indeed doubt of the Miracles
that are faid to attend the Martyrdom, *&c.*
but have no Manner of Doubt concerning
thofe that are attributed to Chrift and his
Apoftles. The Reafon for my doubting
of the one, and believing the other, I am
going to give you. In the former Cafe,
the miraculous Circumftances appear ab-
furd, ridiculous, and unworthy of God,
and this their natural Incredibility in the
Balance of Reafon outweighs all the Teftimony upon Earth. * In the Cafe of the
Gofpel Miracles there is nothing but what
is extremely credible, nothing but what
might be expected from an all-wife and

* See Mr *Bower*'s *Hiftory of the Popes*, Vol. II P 11,
Note under the Letter A

gracious

gracious Being; and when Facts of this Nature come properly attefted, as nothing can be pleaded in Bar to the Teftimony, there is nothing to induce a reafonable Man to with-hold his Aflent.

When the Dr. fays, " that *extraordinary* " or *miraculous* Events are, in the Nature " of them, or as to the Poffibility of their " Exiftence, as credible as *ordinary*;—that " a Man's Senfes are to *himfelf* as good " Evidence of a Miracle as of an ordinary " Event," *&c.* All this we agree to; it feems all to be very true, but happens unfortunately to be nothing at all to the Purpofe: That is, nothing to the Purpofe of proving, that there is the fame Grounds for *paufing* at our Saviour's Miracles, as there is at the Story of *Caftor* and *Pollux* related by *Dionyfius* of *Halicarnaffus*, or the Miracles faid to have happened at *Polycarp*'s Death. That a Man's Senfes enable him to judge of an Event above the common Courfe of Nature, as well as what is according to it, we do not deny.

F 2 When

When a Man of plain common Senfe, of whofe moral Chaiactei we are well affured, attefts a Fact of this Kind, no Way *improbable* in itfelf, we do not object to his Evidence; we only object, when the Atteftation is to a Fact *improbable*; we object, not becaufe he relates a Miracle, but becaufe he relates an *improbable* Miiacle, between which, that is, Things *probable* and *improbable*, human Reafon will make a Diftinction, even where the Atteftations are equal. This Diftinction Dr. *Stebbing* himfelf feems to admit a little afterwards, wheie he fays, " that, in " Things which are to be ieceived upon " Teftimony, the Natuie of the Thing " teftified, and the Quality of the Wit- " neffes, aie to be confidered."—" The " Natuie of the Thing teftified"—That is, in calculating the Force of Evidence, the *Probability* oi *Improbability* of the Thing attefted, is always to be taken into the Account. Tho' a Fact be ever fo well witneffed, yet, if it implies any Thing contrary to what we can conceive of God Almighty,

Almighty, we are bound to reject it; becaufe we have a better Affurance from our
Reafon that it is *falfe*, than we can have
from any verbal Teftimony that it is *true*.
This is the Thing we fay, and infift that,
in Confequence of this Diftinction, we
are at full Liberty to *paufe* at the Miracles faid to have happened at *Polycarp*'s Martyrdom, whilft thofe we find
recorded in the New Teftament, having
every Thing for them, and nothing againft
them, require and demand the full Affent
of our Minds.

It will not, I prefume, be thought
foreign to the Subject, if I hence take Occafion to fay one Word concerning the
Nature of that Evidence upon which a
Miracle in general is to be believed. There
feems to be a good deal of Perplexity
amongft Writers upon this Head, tho'
the Matter, I think, may eafily be difen-
tangled, and made tolerably clear in a few
Words. We will proceed upon the
Foundation Dr. *Stebbing* himfelf has laid.
" A

" A Man's Senfes, fays he, are to himfelf
" as good Evidence of a Miracle, as of an
" ordinary Event," I would afk, does
not this go upon a Suppofition that a Man's
Belief of a Miracle is to be founded upon
the Evidence of Senfe? Do not be in a
Hurry, and miftake me; I do not mean
that it is requifite for every fingle Perfon to
have the Evidence of his own Senfes, and
that no one is concerned to believe any
Fact of this Nature which he does not fee
with his own Eyes; No! my Meaning
only is, that every miraculous Fact, in
order to command my Belief, muft be fup-
ported by the Evidence of fome body's
Senfes or other. If I was not a Witnefs
to it myfelf, my Bufinefs is to enquire
backwards from Age to Age, from Teftimony to Teftimony, 'till I arrive at fome
Perfon who was a Witnefs to it. When
this Witnefs is found, we have then fomething fure and certain to depend upon;
but, 'till this Work is compleated, we are
all in a State of Doubt and Uncertainty.
You will perceive then the Point I am

en-

endeavouring to eftablifh, is this : That
the firft Relator of a Miracle, which is to
be depended upon as authentick, muft
be an Eye-Witnefs of it, he muft not go
upon uncertain Hear-fay, and vulgar Re-
port, but muft be able confidently to
affirm, I was myfelf prefent at the Tranf-
action, and know it to be true upon the
Information of my own Senfes. If there
be any Defect here, like an Error in the
firft Principle, it can never be corrected
afterwards. It matters not thro' how many
Hands a Narration with this original Flaw
in it paffes, or what the Quality of thofe
Hands may be, it will gather no frefh
Supplies of Credit by Time, nor will all
the Learning and Integrity in the World
recommend it to the Belief of an inquifitive
Pofterity. I am under very little Concern
by what Name the Zealots of our Times
fhall pleafe to dignify me, they have fair
Scope for their Cenfure in this Declaration,
that I fhall never give up my Faith to a
Miracle, 'till the full Evidence, here infifted
on, be produced for it.

This

This is the Evidence I require in the Matter of *Healing* by the *Royal Touch*, of which I have lately signified my utter Disbelief. Amidst all the Rubbish I have heard or read upon this Subject, I have never met with one Instance of a Cure, upon which the Mind can confidently and securely rest. In order to an absolute Conviction, the Fact must be proved to me in the following Manner. In the first Place, I must be certified that the Subject, upon whom this Cure is pretended to have been performed, was undoubtedly afflicted with a *scrophulous* Distemper, that he had laboured under it some Length of Time, and had tried human Means without Success. It must be certified that in this Condition he was submitted to the *Touch*, and then that a perfect and compleat Cure instantaneously followed without any Recourse to other Remedies. I say, *instantaneously* followed, because whereever God Almighty thinks fit to interpose by an extraordinary Act of Power, it seems

reason-

reasonable to conclude, that he heals at *once*, and not by *Degrees*, this being a very observable Circumstance in every Case of the like Nature recorded in the New Testament, that the Patient was *immediately made whole*. To these Requisites I must add one more; which is, that he did not in a very short Space relapse again into the same Distemper; because, when a sick Man is miraculously restored to Health, 'tis supposable that God effects it by rectifying the whole Juices of the Body, so that the Person shall be no more liable to fall back into that Distemper, than into any other, or than any other Person who has never been troubled with it.

When an Instance, wherein all these Particulars concur, is certified to me by some Person of unquestionable Credit and Veracity, who was a Witness to the whole Process, *then*, and not 'till *then*, I drop my Pen, and am silent. Nor can it be thought strange that the exactest Proof should on this Occasion be demanded, when the

most

moſt authentick Relations we have left us of the Matter, are filled with ſuch a Variety of Nonſenſe as is enough to make one ſick. For fiſt, the moſt ſtrenuous Advocates of this Powei don't know wheie to fix it; like the Pope's Infallibility, ſometimes it is in one Place, ſometimes in another, and ſometimes, as it were, divided betwixt two. At one Time the Doctrine was that it followed the *Unction*, now comes Mr. *Carte* and tells us, it does not follow the *Unction*, and produces *Ch. Lovel* as an Inſtance of it. Then, as to the *Healing*, ſometimes the Patient was quite cuied, ſometimes half cured, and ſometimes not cured at all. There is a Story in the *Philoſophical Tranſactions*, No. 256 P. 332. of a Woman, who, being tioubled with the Kings Evil, was ſent to *London* to be ſtioaked in King *Charles* the Second's Time, but was never the better, yet Mr. *Greatrakes* the *Iriſh* Stioaker perfectly cured her. Sometimes the Cure was a vaſt While about, and ſometimes, after being compleated, the Humours ſoon

broke

broke out afresh.———There is also a great
Deal of Stuff about the Piece of Gold, if
this happened by any Accident to be lost,
the Distemper immediately returned, and
as soon retired again upon its being found.
Some Instances are related of Persons who,
tho' never touched themselves, were perfectly cured by only borrowing the Gold
of a Neighbour who had been touched.
In such infinite Confusion, what is to be
depended on ? I am inclined to be some-
thing the more scrupulous in this Affair,
upon Account of some troublesome Consequences, from which I see no possible
Method of getting clear, if the Fact be
established. And I apprehend it is, for the
Sake of these very Consequences, absurd
and unreasonable as they are, that the
Belief of it has gained so easy an Admission
into the Minds of my Countrymen.——But
to return.

Thus have I ventured to lay down a
Rule for distinguishing between Miracles
that are to be received as true, and Miracles

that

that may reasonably be doubted, and am
of Opinion it will bring the present Con-
troversy to a short Issue. For Experiment,
let us apply it to the two Cases under Con-
sideration, the Miracles of the Gospel-Age,
and those of after Times. We shall perceive that it will confirm and establish the
one, and set us free from the Necessity of
enlarging our Creed with the other. Whoever but casts his Eye into the Gospel-
Histories, will there find a great Number
of particular Facts so minutely and circum-
stantially described, by those who declare
themselves to have been Eye-Witnesses of
those Facts, that, supposing them to have
been written by the Persons whose Names
they bear, and to be conveyed down to us
in the Manner they were written, (which
is at present not the Question) no Man
who is willing to be determined by Evidence, can entertain the least Doubt of their
Truth and Reality. If we apply the Rule to
the other Case, and examine the Accounts
left us by the Fathers of After-Miracles,
we find nothing of this Nature. Not one

of

of the Writers for the firft Three Hundred
Years, (the Period chiefly infifted upon)
not one of thefe Writers, I fay, upon
whofe Authority the Matter folely depends,
pretend to any fuch certain and infallible
Evidence. We except the Cafe of the
Smyrnæan Letter, where the Credit that
would naturally be due to the Atteftation,
we fuppofe to be entirely fet afide by the
Improbability of the Things attefted. In
a Cafe attended with fuch Circumftances,
we think a Man may honeftly refufe to
truft any body's Senfes but his own.
There is no other Inftance, as I remember,
wherein the warmeft of their Advocates
fay, they have affirmed the Reality of a
Miracle upon their own Knowledge.—As
to the Genuinenefs of their Accounts, I fee
no Reafon to fufpect but that they are
come down to us in as uncorrupted a
Manner, as the Scriptures themfelves are;
fo far therefore we admit of an Equality:
The Difference lies here; the Authors of
the Gofpel-Hiftory have pofitively declared
themfelves Eye-Witnefles of the Facts
they

they relate, the others have declared no
fuch Thing; a Ground of Diftinction that
will eternally fubfift, and eternally defy the
utmoft Efforts of the moft fubtle Objectors.
——And I am perfuaded that, had the
Gofpel-Miracles ftood upon no better a
Foundation than thofe about which
all this Rout is made, the Credit of
them had been deftroyed many Centuries ago, and the Chriftian Religion, that
is built upon them, muft have undergone
the fame Fate, and perifhed with them.
Upon this Spot I fix my Foot; and
make no Doubt but we fhall be able to
maintain the Ground againft the whole
Herd of Unbelievers of every Denomi-
nation. Let them make the moft of the
Notice here given them; they are welcome
to extract what Advantage out of it they
can : It happens that I am not under fo
great Apprehenfions from that Quarter as
Dr. *Stebbing* feems to be, I have at prefent the utmoft Contempt for their Objections, and fhall trouble my Head no
farther about them, 'till I fee fomething
from

from their Hands that may deferve a ferious
Examination.

After all, fuppofing (not granting) that
thefe Gentlemen have a fmall Matter the
better of the Argument, that Victory rather
inclines to their Side, in fhort, that they
have made it fomething more probable that
there *were* Miracles after the Times of the
Apoftles, than that there *were not*; what
does all this amount to? Will this juftify
the Strefs that has been laid upon it?
'Tis well known that fome of our ableft
Divines think it a Queftion of little or no
Moment. Why then is it preffed upon
us, as of that Certainty, and of that Confequence, as tho' a Man could hardly be
a Chriftian without believing it? *——The

* Tho' I cannot agree with Dr *Stelling* in his Reafoning upon this Subject, yet I think it but a neceffary Piece
of Juftice to own, that he has been much fofter and more
moderate upon the Queftion in general, than moft of the
Writers who have appeared againft the *Free Enquiry* In
whom, I will be fo *free* as to fay, (to make Ufe of a Word
much in Fafhion) there is a great Deal of Zeal and Pomp
of Learning, with a very little Knowledge of the Argument

Founda-

Foundations are fapping—The Faith of all History muft go along with it—Ridiculous Outcry! Be it known there are thofe who will undertake to defend Chriftianity better without thefe Miracles, than moft of the Worthies who run away with this Non-fenfe, are able to do with them.—But for God's Sake, my good Friend, where Things are not made very clear, let us not be too hafty in dealing out Anathema's: This is a Branch of Liberality in which I could wifh to fee my Brethren a little more fparing, and think it would be of Service to the Caufe they would fupport; being under fome Temptation to believe that more fubftantial Injury has been done to our Religion by thofe who mean it well, in infifting over-much upon Matters of fmall Importance, and laying a Strefs upon Doctrines beyond either their Utility, or the Evidence there is for them, than by all the mighty Objections that ever fprang from the Heads of its moft inveterate Enemies.

Having

A

LETTER

TO THE

MAYOR and CORPORATION.

OF

D E A L E, in *K E N T*,

In Relation to their OPINION upon the

TRINITY.

L O N D O N.

Printed for J. SHUCKBURGH, at the *Sun*, between
the *Temple-Gates.* MDCCLII.

[Price Six-Pence.]

Having now finifhed what I had to fay, I only beg Leave to interpofe one Word of Caution, that my Meaning may not be miftaken. What I do really mean upon this Subject, I am neither afraid nor afhamed to declare to all Mankind; at the fame Time I am not at all defirous of being thought to mean any Thing that I do not. Be it obferved then, I have no where pofitively laid it down that no Miracle was ever wrought after the Days of the Apoftles. This would be going farther than Reafon will bear a Man out. A negative Propofition muft not be handled fo ungently: To affirm it peremptorily requires a Degree of Confidence I am not yet arrived at. The utmoft I would be underftood to fay is this, that fiom all I have met with, profeffedly written againft the *Free Enquiry*, no clear Evidence comes out, that there was. The Arguments of Dr. *Middleton* are to me of more Force towards inducing a Sufpicion that no miraculous Poweis weie continued to the Chuich, than the Reafoning of all his

H   Oppofers

Oppofers to create any Thing like a firm Belief of the Contrary.

As to thofe who have been ufed to look upon the Gofpel-Miracles, and the Product of fucceeding Ages, in the fame Light, as fo connected and linked together by a Samenefs in the Foundation, that the Deftruction of one muft neceffarily draw after it that of the other, I truft they will now in fome Meafure be fatisfied, that there is a fpecifick Difference difcoverable between them; that the one may be confidered apart and diftinctly from the other; that the former may be foundly and rationally defended, whilft we yield up the latter as the uncontefted Property, nay, as the very Food and Subfiftence of Papifts. I will now releafe you, and am, *S I R*,

Your very affectionate Friend and Servant,

Upton-Grey,
June 20, 1750.   F. TOLL.

⁂ It will be very evident to an attentive Confiderer, that what has here been offered concerning the proper Evi-nence of a Miracle, does not all interfere with the learned
Mr.

Mr. *Warburton's* Argument upon *Julian's* Attempt to rebuild the Temple of *Jerusalem* That divine Providence should interpose to defeat a Scheme projected in manifest Defiance of Jesus Christ, and to give him the Lye, is in itself the most probable Thing in the World, nay, we may go so far as to say, it was really concerned to interpose in Vindication of its own Authority, and if so, why not by those Means which are said to have been employed in it, as well as by any other that can be imagined? That the Design was begun, and not executed, were Facts of publick Notoriety, and when an heathen Writer, who lived at the Time, tells us the Stop was occasioned by the sudden Eruption of Fires from the Foundation, no Reason can be given why we should not take his Word for it He does not relate it as a Miracle, (this a Pagan could not do, his Account therefore the less suspicious) but gives a bare Matter of Fact, as a Reason of the Emperor's desisting from the Enterprize. Which being sufficiently ascertained, the only remaining Question is, whether these Fires can be supposed to have proceeded from natural Causes? Against which we may venture to affirm, there is the odds of several Millions to an Unit.

F I N I S.

Lately publish'd, by the same Author.

A Defence of Dr. MIDDLETON's *Free Enquiry*, against Mr. DODWELL's *Free Answer*.

Price 1 s. 6 d.

CPSIA information can be obtained
at www.ICGtesting.com
Printed in the USA
BVHW04*0318250618
519746BV00025B/56/P

9 781385 504925